Get to Know Your Pet

Dogs and Puppies

JINNY JOHNSON

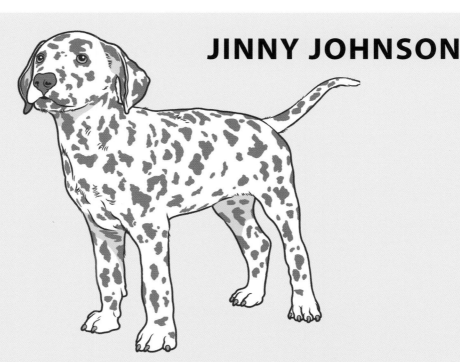

SAUNDERS
BOOK COMPANY

Published by Saunders Book Company
27 Stewart Road
Collingwood, ON Canada L9Y 4M7

Designed by Guy Callaby
Edited by Mary-Jane Wilkins
Illustrations by Bill Donohoe
Picture research by Su Alexander

Thanks to Richard, James, Ella, Simon and Joe
for their help and advice.

Picture acknowledgements
page 4 Naturfoto Honal/Corbis; 5 Paul Barton/Corbis; 6 Robert
Daly/Getty Images; 7 Jim Craigmyle/Corbis; 8 Lynda Richardson/
Corbis; 10 Angela Hampton/RSPCA Photolibrary; 11 Dag Sundberg/
Getty Images; 12 Roy Morsch/Zefa/Corbis; 13 Pat Doyle/Corbis;
14 Herbert Spichtinger/Zefa/Corbis; 17 Dale C. Spartas/Corbis;
18 Steve Lyne/Getty Images; 20 Jim Craigmyle/Corbis; 22 Ariel
Skelley/Corbis; 23 Jim Craigmyle/Corbis; 24 Roy McMahon/Corbis;
25 Dale C. Spartas/Corbis; 27 Photomorgana/Corbis
Front cover Alan & Sandy Carey/Zefra/Corbis

Johnson, Jinny.
     Dogs and puppies / Jinny Johnson.
     p. cm.—(Get to know your pet)
     Includes index.
     Summary:"Describes the behavior of dogs and puppies and
     how to choose and care for pet dogs"—Provided by publisher.
     ISBN 978-1-897563-29-8 pbk
     1. Dogs—Juvenile literature. 2. Dogs—Behavior—Juvenile
literature. I. Title.
SF426.5.J65 2009
636.7—dc22

                                        2007052598

Printed in the United States of America
in North Mankato, Minnesota
092010
DAD0025d

9 8 7 6 5 4

Contents

Dogs–Wild and Tame

For many people, a dog is the perfect pet. Dogs are loyal and friendly, but they do need lots of attention. They shouldn't be left alone in the house all day.

The dogs we keep as pets are probably descended from wolves. Wolves live in family groups called packs and pet dogs are naturally pack animals too. A dog's owners become its pack and a dog has to learn to obey the owner's rules. Dog owners must keep their pets under control at all times when they are out and about and clean up any mess the dogs make.

Early Pets

Experts think that people started to tame wolves about 12,000 to 15,000 years ago. The wolves probably protected their owners and helped them hunt for food.

Wolves live in packs of up to 20 animals, led by a male and female pair.

A dog becomes part of the family and loves to go out with you.

PET SUBJECT

Q **Why does my dog bow down and wag its tail when it sees me?**

A This is a play bow—the dog bows down at the front while keeping its back up and its tail slowly wagging. It may bark at the same time. What your dog is trying to say to you or to another dog is "Come and play with me."

Kinds of Dogs

There are more than 400 different types, or breeds, of dogs. They range from tiny terriers to big dogs such as Labradors, collies, and retrievers. Great Danes, wolfhounds, and German shepherds are even larger.

People breed pedigree dogs to be a particular size or have a particular appearance—or to do certain jobs, such as herd sheep or track things. But many people are happy with a mixed-breed or "mutt" dog, which has parents of different breeds. If you are thinking of choosing a mixed-breed dog, try to find out about both its parents so you know what it might look like when it grows up and how big it is likely to be. That cute little puppy might grow much larger than you expect!

The Irish Wolfhound is one of the biggest breeds of dog, but it is gentle and good with children.

PET SUBJECT

Q **Why does my dog lift its leg when it pees?**

A By lifting its leg as it urinates against a tree or fence, the dog is leaving its pee, and its scent, at about the nose level of other dogs. This means that other dogs are more likely to pick up its scent. Male dogs do this more than females.

Working Dogs

Dogs such as Labradors and golden retrievers can be trained to do a variety of different jobs. Some do important work as guide dogs for blind or deaf people. Dogs can also be trained to work with physically disabled people and can learn to open and close doors, help their owner dress and undress, and even take clothes out of a washing machine.

DOGGY FACT
A guide dog for the blind works for about seven years, then retires to enjoy life as a pet.

Do Dogs Talk to Each Other?

Dogs might not talk like humans, but they have lots of ways of keeping in touch with each other and telling us how they feel.

Dogs make different sounds, from whines and whimpers to growls and loud barks. In fact, one of the first reasons people started to keep dogs was for their warning bark when strangers came near. Dogs bark to warn of possible danger or just to say hello. They whimper and whine to show pain or distress. You will soon learn to understand the various sounds your dog makes.

DOGGY FACT
A dog can hear four times better than we can and can pick up much higher sounds than we can hear.

Dogs howl when they are lonely or nervous. This Brittany Spaniel is howling for attention.

Body Language

Dogs tell us and other dogs how they feel by the way they hold their ears, tail, and body, as well as by barking. A dog that wants to show it is dominant stands up straight with its tail high and looks directly at another dog.

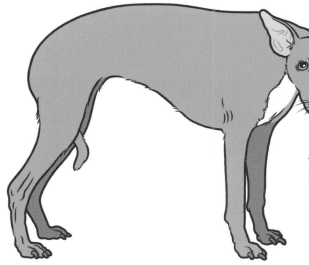

Another dog might show that it is submissive by crouching down, holding its tail low or between its legs, and not looking at the other dog.

PET SUBJECT

Q Why does my dog howl when it is on its own in the house?

A Your dog is trying to get in touch with you. Wolves howl to stay in contact with the rest of the pack or to find their pack members when they are lost. Your dog is doing the same thing—trying to find its pack by howling.

Smelly Signals

For dogs, smell is the most important sense. Dogs have a far better sense of smell than we do and they leave their scent as a signal to other dogs.

As a dog walks along sniffing everything it passes, it is finding a whole world of smells that we do not notice. Watch two dogs meeting. The first thing they do is smell each other. They can tell a great deal from this, such as whether the other animal is male or female, ready to mate, or dominant or submissive.

These dogs are sniffing to find out about each other and say hello.

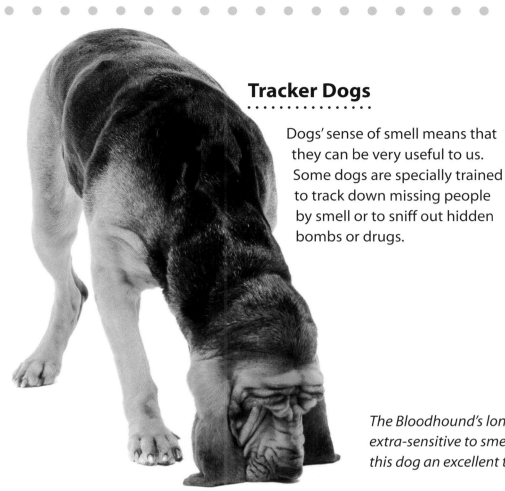

Tracker Dogs

Dogs' sense of smell means that they can be very useful to us. Some dogs are specially trained to track down missing people by smell or to sniff out hidden bombs or drugs.

The Bloodhound's long nose is extra-sensitive to smells, making this dog an excellent tracker.

PET SUBJECT

Q Why does my dog sniff the ground and walk around and around before peeing?

A Your dog wants to find out who's been there before. By sniffing it can discover which other dogs have peed in that spot. It then covers the other dog's smell with its own.

A Dog that's Right for You

When choosing a dog, you first need to decide whether you want a purebred animal or whether you prefer a mutt, or mixed-breed, dog.

The various breeds have different temperaments and not all are right for children. If you want a purebred, choose one that is good with children, such as a collie or a golden retriever. Mixed-breed puppies are usually friendly and good-natured.

Great Danes are very large dogs, but are loving and friendly and make good family pets—if you have lots of room!

Think about what suits you and your family. Do you have space for a big animal? Do you have time to take it out for the exercise it needs every day? A puppy may look cute, but remember to think about how big it might grow. Puppies don't stay small for very long.

Boy or Girl?

Both male and female dogs make good pets. Females are often more obedient and easier to house train. Males may scent mark more and be more aggressive when they meet other dogs. Whichever you choose, it is a good idea to have your dog neutered to avoid unwanted puppies.

PET SUBJECT

Q Why is my dog scared of thunder?

A Lots of dogs are scared of loud noises, such as thunder and fireworks. Remember, their hearing is much better than ours, so these sounds are very loud to them. Always keep your dog indoors during storms or firework displays, and if possible, stay with it to give comfort. Perhaps you could play some music to drown out the sound or play a game with your dog.

Choosing Your Dog

You can buy purebred dogs from breeders or ask whether your vet knows of any litters of puppies. Always ask to see the puppy's mother so you can check that she is fit and healthy.

Another idea is to contact your local rescue center, which will have puppies and adult dogs that need good homes. A rescue center will help you choose the right dog for you and your family. Never buy a dog from a pet store. It might have come from a puppy farm, where puppies are bred but not given enough care and attention.

PET SUBJECT

Q Why does my dog pant?

A Dogs pant to cool down when they are hot. Dogs only have sweat glands on the soles of their feet, so they can't sweat as we do. As a dog pants, it lets cool air into its mouth, which then cools the blood in its nose. This cooled blood travels around the dog's body. Panting also helps to cool the dog's mouth and tongue.

When choosing your pet, remember to find out how big a cute puppy will be when full-grown.

What to Look For

- A healthy, alert animal that doesn't shy away from your touch
- Shiny, clean fur
- Clear, bright eyes
- Ears that are clean and pink inside
- No sign of diarrhea

What Your Pet Needs

Before you bring your new puppy or dog home with you, make sure you have everything it will need to be comfortable.

Buy food and water bowls. Heavy pottery or stainless steel bowls are best, as they can't be tipped over easily. Your dog will enjoy a dog bed—it's a good idea to get your dog used to sleeping there from the start, instead of on the sofa or your bed. You will also need toys, a brush and comb for grooming, a leash and—very important—a poop scoop to pick up the poop.

Chews and toys

Food bowls

Water dish

There might seem a lot to buy for your puppy at first, but most of the equipment will last for a long time.

Bed

Basket

PET SUBJECT

Q **Why does my dog eat its poop?**

A It's normal for animals such as rabbits to eat their poop. But when a dog eats poop, it may be a sign that it is not getting enough of certain vitamins, so check with your vet. Other dogs just like the taste of the poop. Try sprinkling the poop with spicy sauce to make it taste bad. Or just pick it up with your poop scoop before the dog can eat it.

Once your dog can go outside, it must wear a collar with a tag giving your name, address, and phone number. Your vet can also microchip your dog. The microchip is injected into the skin at the back of the neck and has a number that can be read by a special machine. This means that even if your dog loses its collar, it can be identified as yours.

Your dog must wear a collar with a tag showing its name and address when it is outside your home.

Bringing Your Pet Home

Puppies are ready to leave their mom at about eight weeks old. When you first bring your puppy home, try to imagine how it might feel. It will be away from its family for the first time, so it is bound to be nervous.

Be extra gentle and kind during the first days and make sure there are not too many people around or lots of noise. Give your puppy love and attention, but let it rest and get used to its new home, too. Show your puppy where to sleep and eat. An adult dog also needs time to get used to its new home. You might need to be very patient with an adult dog, which might not have had a good home before and may be very anxious.

Your new pet will want lots of love and attention, but remember that it needs its sleep too.

Puppy Pen

One way of helping your new puppy settle in and get used to your family and other animals is to keep it in a puppy pen at first. The puppy should have water, food, some toys, and a comfy bed in the pen. Place the pen where the puppy can see what's going on.

A puppy pen can help your puppy feel safe in its new home.

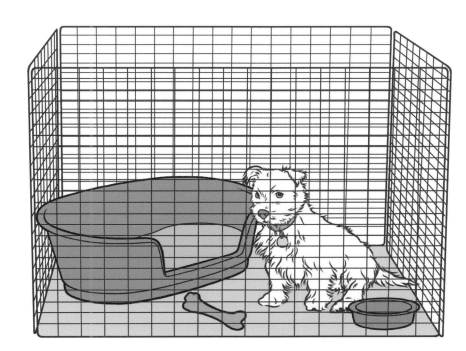

Puppy-Proofing Your Home

● Before your puppy arrives, you and your family need to make sure that your home is safe.
● Don't leave small toys such as plastic building bricks lying around that your dog might choke on.
● Don't leave doors or low windows open—your puppy might get out.
● Check for loose wires that your puppy might chew.
● Make sure any poisonous houseplants are out of reach.

If you let your puppy out into the yard, make sure it can't escape or get into danger.

Feeding Your Pet

Find out what food your pet has been used to, whether it's a puppy or an adult dog. Give it the same food for the first week or so, even if you make changes later.

A puppy needs four meals a day at first, but this can be cut down to three once it is about 12 weeks old. Once your dog is six months old, you can feed it just twice a day—morning and evening.

Check with your vet about how much food your puppy needs.

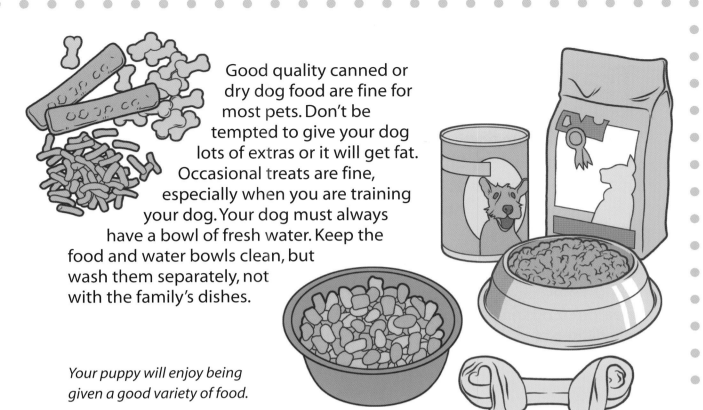

Good quality canned or dry dog food are fine for most pets. Don't be tempted to give your dog lots of extras or it will get fat. Occasional treats are fine, especially when you are training your dog. Your dog must always have a bowl of fresh water. Keep the food and water bowls clean, but wash them separately, not with the family's dishes.

Your puppy will enjoy being given a good variety of food.

PET SUBJECT

Q **Why does my dog have an extra claw on his leg?**

A Dogs walk on their toes, not on the soles of their feet as we do. They walk on four toes. All their toes have claws, but some dogs have a fifth toe a bit higher up that doesn't touch the ground. This is called a dew claw. It might look as though it is on the dog's leg, but this is still part of a dog's foot.

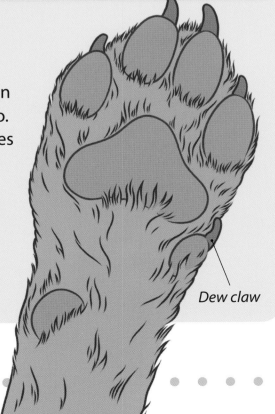

Dew claw

Training Your Pet

Start training right away, so your dog knows what you expect. Changing the rules confuses a dog, so don't let it lie on your bed one day and then shout at it for doing so the next.

The first thing a new puppy has to learn is toilet training. Find a spot indoors that is easy to clean and put down some newspaper. When you think your puppy wants to pee, put it on the paper. If your puppy does something, give it lots of praise. It will soon get the idea.

Be very patient with your puppy when toilet training and give it lots of encouragement.

Once your dog has had all its vaccinations and can go outside, move the newspaper into the yard, then slowly get the dog used to peeing without the newspaper. There will be lots of accidents at first, but never shout at your dog. Puppies are like toddlers—they can't hold it for long.

Your dog will also need to be trained to do things such as sit when you tell it to and to walk by your side. You may like to teach your dog to "shake" when asked.

PET SUBJECT

Q How much sleep does my puppy need?

A Puppies, like babies, need plenty of sleep while they are growing. Once your puppy settles, it should sleep at night when you do and take naps during the day. Don't wake your puppy when it's having a nap. Even full-grown dogs like to sleep during the day and most dogs sleep between 10 and 13 hours a day.

Playtime and Exercise

Dogs love to play and need plenty of exercise. Some kinds of dogs need more exercise than others, so ask your vet for advice.

Remember that young dogs grow fast and get tired quite quickly, so don't try to make a young puppy do too much.

Wearing a Leash

Start getting your puppy used to wearing a leash as soon as possible. Put a collar on for a while every day, then take it off in case it catches on something. Let your puppy get used to walking on a leash at home before taking it out.

All dogs, big or small, need some exercise every day and like to go for walks.

Q Why does my dog chew my shoes?

A Dogs love to chew. It is good for their teeth and gums, particularly when a puppy is growing its second teeth. Your dog can smell you on your shoes and so might find them comforting to chew on while you're not around. Leave your dog some chew toys to play with while you are out.

Playing games such as catch is a great way to exercise your dog.

Your dog will enjoy playing with you and by itself. Buy some soft chewing toys that your dog can play with when it is alone. Activity toys that you put a treat inside are also fun. But best of all is playing with your dog yourself, throwing a ball for him to fetch.

Handling and Grooming

Let your puppy get used to being handled when it is young. Keep your movements slow and gentle so you don't frighten it.

Dogs are good at keeping themselves clean, but even short-haired dogs enjoy being brushed and combed. Some long-haired breeds must be groomed to stop their coats from becoming matted and tangled. Some may also need to have their coats clipped in summer so they don't get too hot. Grooming time also gives you a chance to check your pet's coat for fleas.

Picking Up a Dog

If you need to pick up your puppy or dog, make sure you support it well, with one hand under its chest and the other under the back of its body.

It's a good idea to get your puppy used to being picked up. Always support the dog's body well.

PET SUBJECT

Q **Do dogs like being petted?**

A They do. Dogs are very sensitive to touch and wild dogs in a pack nuzzle and groom each other. Being petted and touched helps a dog feel secure. Most dogs like to be petted on the head and back, but many don't like the tail area being touched. Dogs also have extra-sensitive hairs above the eyes and below the jaws. These pick up tiny movements in the air.

Start cleaning your puppy's teeth as soon as possible, so it gets used to the idea. At first, you can just wipe the teeth or rub them with a rubber finger brush. Then you can start brushing properly with a special dog toothbrush and toothpaste.

A dog's nails need clipping regularly. Ask your vet to do this or to show you how.

For Parents and Caregivers

Caring for any pet is a big responsibility. Looking after an animal takes time and money, and children cannot do everything themselves. You'll need to be prepared to show your child how to behave around the animal, provide what the pet needs, make sure it is healthy, and make sure that it has the necessary vaccinations. You'll also have to organize neutering your puppy when the time comes.

A dog may live for 13 or 14 years or more. Animal welfare organizations say that a dog needs about five hours of attention a day, so you're taking on a big commitment. That said, helping to look after a pet and learning how to respect it and be gentle in handling it are very good for a child and can be great fun too.

CHOOSING A PUPPY OR DOG
Be careful to choose a healthy animal and make sure you choose a dog that is good with children. Whether you go to a breeder or a rescue center, always explain to the person in charge that you want a family pet, and ask their advice. When you first get your puppy or dog, take it to the vet as soon as possible for a health check and advice on vaccinations against diseases such as distemper, infectious canine hepatitis, parvovirus, and others.

Your dog will need booster injections every year. Remember, too, that your new pet will have to stay indoors until it has been vaccinated.

TRAINING
A dog, unlike pets such as cats, goes out with you and mixes with other people and dogs. So it is very important to train your dog to be obedient. It has to learn to behave in a way that is not dangerous or upsetting for others.

Start to show your dog what you expect right away. Ask your vet for advice and try to go to dog training classes. You are responsible for any mess your dog makes, so always carry a poop scoop and a supply of plastic bags. Make sure the whole family follows the rules about handling your dog in public.

FEEDING

You'll need to supervise feeding and buy food, but your child can help, especially when you're feeding dry food. Don't let your child give the dog too many treats. Never give it human treats, particularly chocolate, which is poisonous to dogs and may give them diarrhea. Your child can help to make sure the puppy or dog always has a bowl of fresh water.

TRAVELING WITH YOUR DOG

You may want to take your dog when you go out and you will need to take it to the vet, so it is important to get your dog used to traveling in the car. An unsecured dog can be dangerous in a car accident, so install a dog guard, crate, or dog seat belt to keep the dog safe. Never leave your dog in the car on a hot day. It can be fatal.

If you want to take your dog to another country, it can now have a special dog passport. The dog will need vaccinations and these take time to organize, so start well in advance. If you go away without your dog, you will need to make proper arrangements for its care. Ask your vet or local Humane Society if they can recommend good boarding kennels and make sure you book ahead.

NEUTERING

Pet dogs should be neutered to reduce the numbers of unwanted animals. Neutering is not painful and does not change the animal's personality. Some people believe it is best to let a female have a litter of puppies before neutering, but this is not necessary.

MICROCHIPPING

A dog must wear a collar and tag, but collars can come off and get lost. Most vets and animal welfare organizations now recommend microchipping as a permanent way of identifying your pet. The chip, with a unique number, is injected into the dog's skin at the back of its neck. It is quick, easy, and doesn't hurt. The number on the chip can be read by a scanner and is kept on file at a national database. If your dog gets lost, it can be quickly identified by any vet and brought home.

Glossary

aggressive
An aggressive dog is fierce and likely to fight.

breeder
Someone who keeps purebred dogs and sells the puppies they produce.

diarrhea
A dog suffering from diarrhea has loose, watery poop.

dominant
A dominant dog is a leader.

grooming
To care for and clean a dog's coat by brushing or combing it.

mutt
A dog that is a mix of two or more breeds.

neutering
An operation performed by a vet on a male or female animal so that it cannot have babies.

purebred
A purebred dog is one that is a special type, such as a Beagle or a Bloodhound. A purebred dog has a certificate giving details about its parents.

scent
Another word for smell.

submissive
A submissive dog is content to let other dogs take the lead.

temperament
A dog's natural personality—whether it is fierce or gentle, bouncy or quiet.

urinate
To pee.

vaccination
An injection given to your dog or puppy by the vet to prevent it from catching certain serious illnesses.

vitamins
Substances contained in food that are necessary for good health and help an animal's body work properly.

Web Sites

For Kids:

American Kennel Club Kids' Corner

http://www.akc.org/public_education/kids_corner/kidscorner.cfm

An online newsletter featuring stories about responsible dog ownership, safety, and activities kids and their dogs can participate in.

ASPCA Animaland: Pet Care

http://www.aspca.org/site/PageServer?pagename=kids_pc_home

The American Society for the Prevention of Cruelty to Animals has some excellent advice about caring for your pets.

Care for Animals: Kid's Corner

http://www.avma.org/careforanimals/kidscorner/default.asp

The American Veterinary Medical Association offers activities and worksheets to help kids be responsible pet owners and find out everything they need to know before they get a pet.

For Teachers:

Best Friends Animal Society: Humane Education Classroom Resources

http://www.bestfriends.org/atthesanctuary/humaneeducation/classroomresources.cfm

Lesson plans and lots of information about treating animals humanely.

Education World Lesson Plans: Pet Week Lessons for Every Grade

http://www.educationworld.com/a_lesson/lesson/lesson311.shtml

Use the topic of pets to engage your students in math, language arts, life science, and art.

Lesson Plans: Responsible Pet Care

http://www.kindnews.org/teacher_zone/lesson_plans.asp

Lesson plans for grades preschool through sixth, covering language arts, social studies, math, science, and health.

Index